Faith
It's Voice
Activated

AMELIA NAZER

BALBOA.
PRESS
A DIVISION OF HAY HOUSE

Scripture taken from the Holy Bible, NEW INTERNATIONAL VERSION®. Copyright © 1973, 1978, 1984, 2011 by Biblica, Inc. All rights reserved worldwide. Used by permission. NEW INTERNATIONAL VERSION® and NIV® are registered trademarks of Biblica, Inc. Use of either trademark for the offering of goods or services requires the prior written consent of Biblica US, Inc.

Scripture taken from the New King James Version. Copyright © 1979, 1980, 1982 by Thomas Nelson, Inc. Used by permission. All rights reserved.

Balboa Press books may be ordered through booksellers or by contacting:

Balboa Press
A Division of Hay House
1663 Liberty Drive
Bloomington, IN 47403
www.balboapress.com.au
1 (877) 407-4847

Print information available on the last page.

ISBN: 978-1-5043-0480-1 (sc)
ISBN: 978-1-5043-0481-8 (e)

Balboa Press rev. date: 11/04/2016

This book is dedicated to you, its reader.
May your faith declare the promises of His Word.

Acknowledgements

Thank you to my husband, Byron, for his support and for always believing in me.

I want to thank my gorgeous children, Bianca, Ayron, and Megon.

Thank you Jacqueline Mannie and Bernadine Burrel for your friendship.

I want to thank Ethel Adams and Joan Malgas for their guidance and support.

I will always be thankful to my late mother, Sybil Marongo, for making me the woman I am today.

My greatest gratitude goes to God. Thank you, Father, for the opportunity to share Your Word. Thank you for Your visitations. I am immensely grateful for the opportunity to serve you, and I give You all the glory and all the honour.

And they heard the sound of the Lord God walking in the garden in the cool of the day. Then the Lord God called to Adam and said to him, "Where are you?" So he said, "I heard Your voice in the garden and I was afraid, because I was naked and hid myself."

—Genesis 3:8–10 NKJV (New King James Version)

Your words were found, I ate them, and Your word to me was the joy and rejoicing of my heart. For I am called by Your name, O Lord God of Hosts.

—Jeremiah 15:16 NKJV

"As for me, this is my covenant with them," said the Lord, "My spirit is on you and my words, which I have put in your mouth, shall not depart out of your mouth, nor out of the mouth of your seed's seed," said the Lord, "from now on and forever."

—Isaiah 59:21 NIV (New International Version)

Contents

Contents

Introduction

Faith—It's Voice Activated

I believe that the power within us is voice activated. God's power is in us, and this power is waiting for us to start the conversation. We are empowered when we read and speak His Word. God gave us a command to call things forth that be not as if they were (Romans 4:17 NKJV).

We activate our faith by speaking it out. Something powerful must happen when we release the Word of God as a declaration. When we call things forth, we activate the power of God within us. This power in us only works when we have a personal relationship with the Creator. The universe is waiting on our every command. Have you received your healing, your new house, or your car? It is waiting for you; it is already done. It requires your faith mixed with the action of speaking it out; faith is voice activated.

Everything God commanded was done. He said, "Let there be light." God gave us a command in Joshua 1:8 (NKJV):

"that this book of the law shall not depart out of thy mouth, but thou shall meditate on it day and night, that thou may observe to do according to all that is written therein: for then thou shall make thy way prosperous, and then thou shall have good success." The spoken word is life changing, because your words have power to change the atmosphere and your circumstances. If you want to see change in your life, start saying something about the Word of God.

In today's busy world, we may face challenges that seem unmanageable; therefore, we need the powerful life-changing spoken Word. When we decree or speak the Word, it can uplift our spirits as we hold on to the promise. As believers, when we speak out about key areas of concern in our lives, we expect breakthrough to manifest, because God's Word will not return void. Just think of your key card: you must activate the card before you can withdraw or deposit money. It is the same with your healing or finances. Speak out your concerns, because faith is voice activated.

The words you speak have power for good or bad, and when you proclaim God's Word in faith, it is activated to bring change in your life. We have the promise in Isaiah 55:11 (NKJV) that His Word does not return empty but accomplishes everything it is sent to do. If God said it, He will do it.

"May these words of my mouth and this meditation of my heart be pleasing in your sight, Lord, my rock and my redeemer" (Psalm 19:14 NIV).

Chapter 1

Our Relationship with Jesus

Human beings are social beings, and they all need contact with each other, which means relationships. The kingdom of God is based on relationships. In the Bible we see that Jesus's theology was based on relationships, and we see that everything with God comes from and through a relationship with Him. We receive blessings through our relationship with God, and it is a starting point where we live and walk from. When we pray the Our Father it demonstrates the relationship between the Father and Son (Matthew 6:9 NKJV). A relationship with no commitment is short-lived; it cannot last. Both parties must willingly agree to the relationship.

The psalmist recognises the importance of relationship as he declares in Psalm 95:1–3 (NKJV), "O come let us sing unto the Lord; let us make a joyful noise to the rock of our salvation. Let us come before His presence with thanksgiving and make a joyful noise unto Him with psalms. For the Lord is a great God and a great King above all gods."

In our relationships with one another, we should have the same mind set as Christ Jesus (Philippians 2:5 NKJV).

A relationship involves two or more people, and it needs commitment in order to have value. Every relationship is based on communication. Christianity is all about relationship; Jesus said, "If you abide in Me, and my word abide in you" (John 15:7 NKJV). The Bible clearly states that we are called by God into a relationship with Him. It is an invitation to have fellowship with Him. God said, "I have loved thee with an everlasting love, therefore with loving kindness have I drawn thee" (Jeremiah 31:3 NKJV).

Jesus came to earth to have a relationship with us. Therefore, our relationship with Him should be our main priority in life. We can only know God through experience, and this experience comes from a relationship with Jesus. When we stay in close communication with God, it generates a relationship of power. We bear fruit when in relationships, and it gives us an opportunity to glorify Him. There is no other name under heaven given among humankind by which we can be saved, and His name is Jesus (Acts 4:12 NKJV).

Trust and Acceptance in the Relationship

A childlike relationship starts with trust; children never worry how their needs will be met. They believe and trust their parents and naturally enjoy the benefits of being children. Jesus wants us to be like little children with no boundaries, no secrets, and no pretence. We have the promise in Jeremiah 17:7 (NKJV); we see that blessed is the person who trusts in Him and whose confidence is in Him. We must come expectantly, knowing as a child of the Most High that all our needs are already met. A parent's hand is always outstretched to comfort a hurting child, to wipe away tears, and even kiss the spot where it hurts. Jesus wants to do the same for us. He is omnipresent—always present; He is every place at the same time. As a father, He loves us, protects us, and heals and comforts us in times of need.

In the Bible Jesus talks about an earthly father who knows how to give good gifts to his children. So our Father also wants to bless and give us good gifts. He taught His disciples to pray, "Our Father, who art in Heaven," in Matthew 6:9–12 (NKJV) for this reason; we commit ourselves and accept Him as our Father.

When a couple decides to marry, they trust each other and make a vow to support each other throughout their marriage. When we trust someone, we give more of ourselves; we confide in our spouses or friends. When there is trust in a relationship, we expect that the other person will be there in our times of need and difficulty. Everything from God comes through a relationship with Him, the Creator. I remember waking up one morning with this scripture in my mind: "Call upon my name and I will answer thee." It was God, asking me to trust Him.

Friendship in the Relationship

The friendship of the Lord is for those who fear Him, and He makes known to them His covenant. The Bible reminds us that a friend sticks closer than a brother (Proverbs 18:24 NKJV). A friendship can only last if there is mutual understanding and agreement.

A relationship with God allows us to walk daily with Him. We pray, we ask, and we worship the Creator of the universe. Everything that we have or want in life comes through our friendship with Jesus. Most people have at some point heard about Jesus and the Bible. Most children who were raised in Christian homes attended Sunday school. They learned about Jesus and His life on earth through illustrated pictures and nativity plays. The birth of Christ is a celebrated worldwide event for believers as well as nonbelievers. We celebrate Christmas by exchanging gifts, and His birth is regarded as a joyous event. Most people are aware that Christmas is all about Jesus.

As believers, we realise that there is a difference between knowing who Jesus is and knowing about Jesus. Having a relationship with our Creator is to *personally* know Him, but religion is to know things *about* Him. When we know who He is, we enter into a relationship with Him. We may know about our Creator through others talking about our heavenly Father. Each of us should ask himself or herself, "Do I *know* Jesus, or do I know *about* Jesus?" When we know who Jesus is, we hunger after a personal relationship with Him. Abraham believed God, when he was told that his descendants would be too numerous to count (James 2:23 NIV).

A relationship with Jesus is the best relationship you can ever have in life. Jesus came to earth to restore the relationship that was lost when Adam sinned. In any relationship, you must invest quality time with each other, because you both have chosen the relationship. It is important to search your own heart, be honest with God, and tell Him exactly how you feel. When you accept the friendship of Jesus, you must have the honesty, boldness, and innocence to ask the Father anything. As Jesus's friend, you are made righteous and have an opportunity to hear from heaven.

Any relationship involves a process of growth, and we grow when there is mutual trust and understanding. It's the same with Jesus, when we receive salvation. It's a process to become holy as He is holy. We should continue to seek the things above. We should seek heaven because our life depends on it (1 Corinthians 3:1 NKJV).

Worship in the Relationship

In worship, we adore our Father, sing praises to His name, and glorify Him for everything we receive. When we worship, we have the opportunity to bless God and declare His greatness and glory. We open a portal of blessings when we worship Him, although the reward should not be our main focus. God will and must turn his attention to us if we worship Him; we are commanded to bless the Lord our God (Deuteronomy 8:10 NKJV).

When we give our lives to Jesus, we take a journey to discover who He really is. To intimately know Jesus, we must desire to worship Him. Our worship is an acknowledgement that we serve and adore the Creator. We have this promise that, if we confess with our mouths that Jesus is Lord and believe in our hearts that God raised Him from the dead, we will be saved (Romans 10:9 NIV). When we talk or pray to Him every day, we desire to bless Him. When we pursue relationships of worship with Jesus, we acknowledge that He is first in our lives, and we enter into a dimension of His holiness. When we have fellowship with Jesus, our Creator reveals Himself to us, and we see Him through the visible creation of nature everywhere we go and look.

As believers, we often receive the Word of God, but He wants us to know who Jesus is. He wants to talk to us directly, and He needs our praise and worship at all times. Jesus wants to meet us on the mountaintop, and He has given us permission to go up the mountain by ourselves. All that is required of us is that we be present when He meets us there.

It is there that we present ourselves to Him, just as we are. Jesus doesn't need explanations about what we have done; He knows us in our entirety. He will only come if we first seek Him and, in worship, we seek first the kingdom of God and His righteousness. Our worship should be the most important thing we do each day, as we enter into His presence. We must bless and praise the Lord our God for all good things received. In worship, we must magnify His holy name and come expectantly to minister unto Him. In worship we must come as we are, despite our circumstances and needs.

Fellowship in the Relationship

I remember clearly the day that I had an encounter with God. I am sure I'd had many before, which had gone unnoticed because of my everyday busy lifestyle. But that day God interrupted my plans. An encounter with God usually happens when you least expect it. I was driving home this day, when suddenly I looked at the cross (rosary) I had hanging from my rear-view mirror. It has been there for a long time, but that day it attracted my attention. I took the cross in my hand and suddenly saw the image of Jesus being crucified. I said out loud, "Lord, I am sorry that you had to suffer on the cross for my sins." As I wept out of gratitude that Jesus was crucified for my sins so that I can have eternal life, I had an overwhelming feeling that I wanted to know more about Jesus. My intimate relationship with Jesus started that day. I became hungry to know about my Saviour. The Bible became my new book and guide to discover who my King was.

The Holy Spirit will pursue us and teach us when we willing to have fellowship with Him. Even though I had already had two visions from God, this was very different. My dreams were comforting, yet this encounter gave me a chance in my brokenness to acknowledge that Jesus is Lord, to confess, repent, and surrender completely.

If you have fellowship with the Creator, He can work through you, in you, and with you to fulfil His Word. God normally uses people to bless you, so that you can be a blessing to many, and His favour is for life (Psalm 30:5

7

NKJV). When you have fellowship with Jesus, it does not mean that there will be no trials or temptations. There will always be challenges and storms, but He will be with you through them all, if you call upon His name.

When you have fellowship, the Father reveals your purpose and destiny to you. Fellowship allows you to enter into a deep level of worship, and God's spirit draws you. It is my experience that you then desire the Lord with all your heart. When you have fellowship with God, He will raise you up into a new spiritual realm.

Growth in the Relationship

Just as in our relationships with family and friends, we know that to maintain or allow the relationship to grow we must spend time with each other. We make an effort to invest in the relationship, for mutual benefit.

It is the same with Jesus; if you want an intimate relationship, you need to pursue him. You must seek His presence. All relationships involve a two-way process; this is how you stay connected. It is seen as spending time with the Lord in prayer and worship.

As you grow in the relationship, you begin to understand that your role is to bless the Lord, and you lose sight of what you want Him to do for you. Jesus said in scripture, "Call upon me and I will show you great and mighty things" (Jeremiah 33:3 NKJV). It is important that you humble yourself before the Lord and be honest and open. Tell God,

"I can't do this on my own. I need your help, Lord, to do your will." You must become passionate to desire the things of God. The Father helps us, and His Grace is sufficient for us and His strength is made perfect in our weakness (2 Corinthians 12:9 NKJV).

Our faith can grow. We read about Naaman the leper, who was a wealthy man. When he was told to wash in the Jordan seven times, he turned away angrily. After his servant spoke with him, he agreed to go and dip in the Jordan (2 Kings 5 NKJV). This man got faith on the way and was healed; we can see that faith grows exceedingly.

Prayer in the Relationship

Prayer is our gateway to heaven. We have access to God twenty-four hours per day, seven days a week. Our technology is so advanced, with Wi-Fi hotspots at major shopping centres and airports, but we need to be connected to use it freely. Access to heaven is wireless and free. There is no time limit or expiry date, and we can pray as often as we choose. Many of us pray out of desperation for our needs when we are in crisis, but the Father will always wait on us to seek Him.

Our prayer life produces power, and we must make prayer a part of our lifestyles. We can start praying for simple things each day. For example, to pray before a meal can become a habit. God hears every single prayer. The great thing about prayer is that we can do it anywhere, anytime, and in any position. We can talk to God while driving or doing our daily chores. One morning I woke up with this verse on my mind: "Call upon my name, and I will deliver thee." It felt as though someone had just read it aloud to me. At times I have awakened and felt as though I had been praying all night. Sometimes when I wake up during the night I will pray until I fall asleep again.

It is important that we engage in an attitude of prayer throughout the day. Prayer is asking for what we need for ourselves or others. We also give praise, worship, and thanksgiving, honouring God for everything. Jesus said, "I will never leave you nor forsake you" (Hebrews 13:5 NKJV).

We can talk to our Father as often as we want. He is always available, and heaven does not close. In our relationship, we must be honest and humble before God. We should genuinely strive to seek His face and not His hand. When we surrender and become completely dependent on God, we have a desire to seek His face daily. God instructs us to "Seek first the kingdom of God and His righteousness, and all these things shall be added to you" (Matthew 6:33 NKJV).

When you realise who your Father is, you don't have to worry about His hand or what He can do for you. God is our provider; He knows what we need before we ask (Matthew 6:8 NKJV). Prayer always keeps us connected to God, and it can change our circumstances. God is timeless; what may seem to us a long time for answering of prayers is like minutes to Him.

When we abide in the presence of the Lord, He helps and hears us. In the book of Psalms, we see that David expressed all his emotions when he came before God. He expressed his anger, love, hate, frustration, and love. David was in tune with his feelings and expressed them; Jesus wants us to do the same when we seek His face. God promised that we would hear His voice in the morning (Psalm5:3 NKJV). Hearing His voice compels us to seek Him. Our Father is ready and waiting to serve our every need. We must continue to be strong in the Lord, not depending on our own strength but realising that we need to depend on God's power.

Thanksgiving in the Relationship

When we love the Lord with all our hearts, which is the first commandment, our desire is to serve Him, and this motivates us to seek His presence at all times. We should start each day by seeking first His kingdom and giving Him thanks. When we enter into His presence, we have a longing to surrender all our worries and problems. When we are in a state of brokenness, we offer Him our praise and worship. We bless and give Him thanks. "Bless the Lord, O my soul" (Psalm 103:1 NKJV). We want to always enter into His presence with expectancy and thanksgiving.

We seek His face to experience an encounter with the Holy One. In Psalm 103:13 (NKJV), we are reminded that the Lord is like a Father to His children, tender and compassionate to those who fear Him. We must thank Him for all things. Just think of five things you have in your house that you can thank Him for. I am sure you can give thanks for all the comfort of electrical appliances and the hot water that is readily available in your kitchen. It is the small things that we take for granted. Name them one by one, and you will be surprised to see how blessed you are.

We must enter into His gates with thanksgiving (Psalm 100:4 NIV), and we desire to come expectantly to minister to Him. The psalmist sings that it is good to give thanks to the Lord and to sing praises to His Name most high. We also declare His loving-kindness in the morning and His faithfulness every night (Psalm 92:1–2 NKJV).

Obedience in the Relationship

When we love God, we will obey His teachings. Jesus tells us in scripture that if we love Him we will obey Him (John 14:15 NKJV). To love the Lord is to follow, trust, and obey Him. Jesus will never disappoint us when we call on His name and He gives us an opportunity to hear from heaven. The more time we spend in His presence or seeking His face, the more sensitive we become to His voice. In our relationship with our Father, He talks to us through scripture, pictures, words, people, or worship. It is an opportunity for the Lord to present to us what He has prepared for us. Jesus says that a man can receive nothing except it be given him from above (John 3:27 NKJV).

As believers, we willingly strive to be obedient and to do the will of God. When His children remain faithful and obedient, God blesses us. As we meet daily with Jesus, we discover that we have a friend in Him. He will never disclose our secrets to the world. He invites us to cast our burden on Him, and He promises to sustain us (Psalm 55:22 NKJV). God gave us the Ten Commandments as a guide to remaining faithful and obedient.

The presence of God can manifest in our lives in different ways, when we worship Him. We don't have to look for God. He always turns up; he is always present, whenever we are willing to hear from Him. It is important to realise that our feelings do not indicate His presence. As believers, we need to become hungry for God, so that He can reveal His glory to us. We have an opportunity to see who Jesus is when we are obedient to him (Philippians 3:10 NKJV). Our Father wants us to know Him, the power of His resurrection, and the fellowship of His suffering. Just as parents reward their children when they are obedient, so the Father blesses and rewards those who worship him.

Honour in the Relationship

We honour God by giving Him our best, and we should give our Father our full attention. When you decide to spend time with the Father, you should never be in a rush. If you are not a morning person, set time aside at night or when it is convenient for you to spend quality time in His presence. Honour requires excellence at all times; you should not honour God because you have needs, but you must do all things for God out of honour. When we honour God, He gives us access to people, things, and places. Honour is a mark of spiritual maturity; it is not fear to do the right thing. It is important to develop an attitude of honour. Just as we honour our parents, leaders, or employers, we honour Jesus because we love Him.

We can practise honour until it becomes a revelation to us. Honour can restore many relationships; it is important to let others know that they are valued. God needs us to acknowledge Him for His greatness. Many of our blessings are a result of honour; we are blessed when we have a family, a job, or a marriage, and we must thank God for what He has given us. The fear of the Lord is the instruction of wisdom, and before honour is humility (Proverbs 15:33 NKJV).

Faith in the Relationship

As believers, we are encouraged to have faith in God and to centre our lives in Him (Mark 11:33 NKJV). Once we seek His presence, an encounter with Jesus will change our perspective on who He is, and this will take us into a new spiritual dimension of His goodness and glory. The Bible reminds us that a relationship including fear of the Lord is just the beginning of an experience of His goodness.

When we seek Jesus, our relationship goes from strength to strength, and He reveals Himself to us. We learn and discover how great our God is. When we enjoy an intimate relationship with Jesus, He helps us to stay focused on what is true, noble, and just (Philippians 4:8 NIV). When we meditate and read the Bible to explore God's promises, we receive revelation. God told Joshua: "This book of the law shall not depart out of thy mouth, but thou shall meditate on it day and night" (Joshua 1:8).

As followers of Jesus Christ, we live in a real world, with real stressors, and we experience everyday pressures of life. We need boldness to conquer the trials and tribulations we face in all seasons of our lives. Jesus is the answer to everything we need in life, and He is the way, the truth, and the life (John14:6 NKJV). Jesus is our gateway to life with God, the Creator of heaven and earth. The only way to a relationship with our heavenly Father is through Jesus Christ, because there is no other name under heaven by which you can be saved (Acts 4:12 NIV).

Forgiveness and Repentance in the Relationship

When we enter into a relationship, it always starts with repentance. When we enter into prayer and forgive others, our Heavenly Father also forgives us (Mark 11:25 NKJV). When we forgive others, we heal ourselves, and the weight of unforgiveness disappears. It is important to repent throughout the day or as soon as we realise that we have sinned. The Bible instructs us to always ask forgiveness before we request anything from the Lord.

Our relationship grows with Jesus when we completely trust Him. We learn to abide in Him. John 15:7 NKJV says, "If you abide in Me, and My words abide in you, you will ask what you desire, and it shall be done for you." We see that

Jesus had a relationship with His disciples, but He knew Judas would betray Him (John 18:2 NIV). He knew who would deny Him (Mathew 26:34 NIV). Just as Jesus knew all about His disciples, He also knows everything about us, our every thought, desire, and fear. "When you come praying, forgive others, just as your heavenly Father forgive you" (Mark 11:25 NKJV).

Spiritual Power in the Relationship

When we have an intimate relationship with the Lord, we receive the rights of a son (John 1:12 NKJV). Our role to maintain this inheritance involves seeking His presence every day. You will receive spiritual power every time you come out of your prayer closet. What a promise we have in the book of Daniel 11:32 (NKJV)! We see that people who know their God by experience shall be strong and carry out great exploits; they shall fight back. With this power in the relationship, we are able to withstand any evil, because power comes out of closeness with God and the Holy Spirit. Jesus said in scripture, "You shall receive power when the Holy Spirit comes upon you" (Acts 1:8 NKJV). The Holy Spirit power gives us boldness to do all things, because this power resides in us.

We also have this promise of power: "Now unto Him that is able to do exceedingly abundantly above all that we ask or think, according to the power that works in us" (Ephesians 3:20 NKJV). We can clearly see that the limit to release the power is not from God but depends on each one of us. With this power of God, we are equipped for spiritual warfare. The power resides within us.

We have power in action through relationship, by living in faith. The more we pray and read God's Word, the more our faith and power is increased and we believe that all things are already done. When we have received this power, we will be transformed by the renewal of our minds and will do things that are good, acceptable, and in the perfect will of God. Jesus said, "Be ye Holy as I am Holy (1 Peter 1:16 NKJV). Our Father also gave us dominion over the earth, which is inherited power.

God gives us a promise in Psalm 30:5 (NKJV), where He states that His favour is for life. We can pray to God and ask Him to show us who He is and ask to have an encounter with Him. Try praying this: "Father, I want to know you more intimately. Help me and give me strength to always seek you first. You said those that seek the Lord shall not lack any good thing (Psalm 34:10 NKJV). The good things in life are just an added blessing if you seek Him first. The psalmist cried out to God, "When you said, 'Seek my face,' my heart said to You, 'Your face, Lord, will I seek'" (Psalm 27:8 NKJV).

Gratitude in the Relationship

When we earnestly seek the presence of the Lord, we should maintain an attitude of gratitude. David described his gratitude thus: "My heart is overflowing with a good theme.

I recite my composition concerning the King; my tongue is the pen of a ready writer" (Psalm 45:1 NKJV).

When Jesus heard that John had been beheaded in prison; He went alone to pray and enter into the Father's presence. Sometimes we don't feel like entering into fellowship, but we should never let feelings keep us from seeking His face. Although Jesus was distraught at this news, He still healed people on that day. Our feelings should never allow us to lose sight of who God is. I believe that we should remain thankful despite what's happening around us. Our Creator promised to be our refuge in times of need.

I remember my very first dream from God. I was taking a nap during the day, and in this dream I saw Jesus on a white cloud, and my mother was with Him. I immediately cried out to her. I called out to my mother and wanted her to stay with me. Then Jesus said to me, "She is safe; she is with me." I could never understand this dream, but since I decided to pursue a personal relationship with Jesus, I now realise that He knew my pain over losing my mother at such a young age, and He came to comfort me. I was very grateful for this visitation; it eased my grief and allowed me to accept that I needed to move on with life, without my mother. When we are in a relationship with Jesus, we can have complete confidence that God is for us. If God is for us, who can be against us? (Romans 8:31 NKJV). We should always have thankful hearts and should acknowledge the Father's goodness in our lives.

Put God First in the Relationship

In our daily walk with Jesus, we desire to seek first the kingdom of God. When we are in a relationship with Jesus, He gives us power to do all things. We realise that an attitude of innocence and trust is important in the relationship. We all know that children are carefree and full of life and that a parent will always put the children first—for example, making sure they have a meal to eat. The psalmist recognises that His "word is a lamp unto my feet and a light unto my path" (Psalm 119:105 NIV).

If we continue to make God the priority in our lives, He acknowledges this by giving us good gifts. We go through a process, and we realise that God must come first, as He is our provider. It is important to start each morning with repentance, to ask forgiveness, and to forgive others.

When we have a need for food or feel hungry, we either prepare a meal or buy takeaway food. We go to any length to satisfy our basic need for food. To seek His face should be the first thing we do each day, and we would then recognise that everything else will fall into place. Worship allows us to enter into His presence; we can ask God to saturate us with His presence. Our brokenness and humble attitude opens the door for our Father to bless us, and when we make Jesus a priority in our lives, He reveals His presence to us through scripture.

Identify Yourself in the Relationship

Even though we can identify with the life of Jesus on earth, it is easy to become familiar with Him. Many of us have either read or heard about His goodness and His character, but knowing all this does not mean we have a relationship with Him. The twelve disciples walked with Jesus, but we see in Mark 8:29 (NKJV) that Jesus asked them, "Who do they say I am?" He knew that even though they followed Him, they actually didn't know who He really was. The Holy Spirit revealed the answer to Peter.

Sometimes we may volunteer in church, but although this is all good deeds, it should not replace our personal relationship with our Creator. Some people take up all these roles to keep busy or to give a good impression of them being good stewards for the kingdom.

Our motives should be clear when we serve in church. The ultimate goal is to be a servant for the kingdom. What would happen if Jesus walked past and you failed to recognise Him? We read in the Bible the story of Mary and Martha; one was busy doing, and one was being. Martha was serving Jesus and His friends; she was doing things for Jesus, while Mary was anointing his feet with expensive perfume. Mary enjoyed spending time with Jesus. Will excessive time spent doing things for Him matter if you miss out on spending quality time with Him? Although it is good and important to volunteer in church, we must be careful not to get caught up in doing things for God and then miss out on who God wants to be for us. We must keep in mind that it is all about our personal walk with the Lord, and we were made by Him and for Him (Colossians 1:16 NKJV).

Jesus Never Changes

God is always looking and waiting for us to seek Him. "God, look down from heaven upon the children of man to see if there is anyone who understands, who seeks God." Our Father is omnipresent and omniscient, but he will never invade where He is not welcome; He will wait patiently for us to come to Him. Jesus remains the same today, yesterday, and forever; He never changes, but he will change us to become Holy as He is holy. Once we have discovered what a relationship with Jesus is all about, it is almost impossible to start each and every day without Him. We change what we thought was important and give God first place. In our walk with Jesus, it is important to cast our cares and leave them at His feet; we must not pick them up again.

In our relationships with Jesus, we should have a longing for God. The psalmist cries out to God as He seeks Him (Psalm 63:1–5 NKJV).

1. O God, you are my God, and I long for you. My whole being desires you; like a dry, worn out and waterless land, my soul is thirsty for you.
2. Let me see You in the sanctuary; let me see how mighty and glorious You are.
3. Your constant love is better than life itself, and so I will praise you.

4. I give you thanks as long as I live; I will raise my hands to you in prayer.
5. My soul will feast and be satisfied, and I will sing glad songs of praise to you.

If you want to be in the presence of God, it is important to learn to seek Him first. In scripture we have the promise that God will make us full of glory in His presence (Acts 2:28 NKJV).

If you want to start a relationship with Jesus, here is a life-changing prayer to ask Jesus to be your Lord and Saviour.

Father, I believe that you sent Your Son to die on the cross for my sins. I accept Jesus Christ as my Lord and Saviour. Forgive me of all my sins; cleanse me with your precious blood. Today I give my life to you; I forgive myself and everyone that I have hurt in the past. I promise to follow you all the days of my life. Amen.

Chapter 2

Visions and Dreams

Vision is defined as the state of being able to see or the ability to think about or plan the future with imagination or wisdom.

To achieve our dreams, we must first desire something. The desire must be something we can measure, for example a house, a car, or a holiday. Some of us may have a desire to start our own ministry. God also gives us desires, and we must have visions and dreams to fulfil our purpose in life, and we see that God will give us our heart's desire (Psalm 21 NKJV).

Write Down Your Vision

Once you have determined what your desire or vision is, you must write it down. We see that God gave clear instructions to Habakkuk: "And the Lord answered me and said, 'Write the vision and make it plain upon the tables, that he may run that read it. For the vision is yet for an appointed time, but at the end it shall speak and not lie, though it tarry, wait for it; it will not tarry'" (Habakkuk 2:2–3 NKJV).

When we write down our visions, they will motivate us. We should focus on God to realise our dreams. We are encouraged to set our hearts on God and hark unto the voice of the Lord. God gave us the promise that all things are possible to those who believe (Mark 9:23 NKJV). It is important, in your vision, to see who you are in Christ. All promises are potentially yours, but you must act on them by meditating on scripture.

Once you have written down your vision or dream, you don't have to know how and when it will come to pass; you must have faith in God to bring it to pass. Our God-given desires will prompt us to explore the paths to greatness. Visions and dreams don't have to be big; they can be simple and small, yet life changing. For example, you may have a desire to start a connect group in your church or join the voluntary team who assist the elderly with shopping once a week.

A vision or dream will motivate you to achieve the impossible; it will allow you to claim by faith and know that God will bring it to pass. The Bible tells us to be specific with our visions. In the book of Genesis, we see that God asks Hagar, "What do you want?" Sometimes we have many desires at the same time, and there is nothing wrong with desiring a car, a house, and a business at the same time, but these may manifest at different times in your life.

Inspired Desires

Sometimes desires are motivated by what you have seen on television, or you may have heard a conversation at work or church that inspires you to act on it. A simple advertisement can inspire someone to invent something. When you receive a revelation, find a scripture on—for example—invention, and meditate on it until it comes to pass. You serve a big God, so you must take the limits from God. Just ask, and dream big—you are not going to bring it to pass. The earth is the Lord's and the fullness thereof, the world and those who dwell in it (Psalm 24:1 NIV).

Ask the Lord to bless your plans, and you will be successful in carrying them out (Proverbs 16:3 NKJV).

Change Your Thoughts

If you have a vision or dream, it allows you to think and see differently. You are encouraged to take a leap of faith into the unknown. Sometimes you wait for miracles to happen for yourself, but sometimes it is better to be a miracle for others. Repentance changes the way you see or take in reality, and it is important to know that God will bring all your desires to pass. Your job is to believe that He can and He will—because all His promises are *yes* and *Amen*.

God promises victory whenever you meditate on scripture: "He did not waver at the promises of God through unbelief but was strengthened in faith by giving glory to God. And being fully convinced that what He had promised, He was also able to perform (Romans 4:20–21 NKJV). Any declaration based on scripture will renew and change your atmosphere, and when you meditate on the Word of God it will open the heavens and change the course of your circumstances to align with the will of God.

Vision Requires Trust

We see that people without visions perish (Proverbs 29:18 NKJV). If we have visions, this allows us to trust God and see the invisible now. Our Lord wants us to prosper, but a promise from God requires faith. Ask yourself, "What am I thinking about? Can I see the impossible now?" We all know that God is timeless; time was invented for man. As a man thinks in his heart, so is he (Proverbs 23:7 NKJV).

We are commanded to meditate on God's Word day and night. The Bible says that when the heart is full the mouth speaks. The heart and the mouth are connected, and faith is voice activated. It is important to be specific, to say out loud what your dreams are and when you want to achieve them. When we confess the Word, the Word of God increases, and we can be sure that God can turn any situation around. It is important to write out the exact details of what you want to achieve. Be specific in your desires, think about it as often as you can and create a mental picture of what you want to achieve.

When we focus on God continuously, or as often as we can throughout the day, our hearts store His promises. I believe it is in our hearts that we change our thinking. Our emotions are stored in our hearts, and this is where feelings of doubt and disappointment occur. If we remain positive and seek the Lord daily, we learn how to slowly die to the flesh. Ask yourself, "What am I speaking over myself? Is what I am saying about myself, building me up?"—because what we say we become.

The Bible tells us what we can have; it is full of God's promises. God works through visions and dreams. He even downloads dreams and desires to us while we sleep, when we trust Him. We are encouraged not to throw away our confidence, because it has a great recompense of reward (Hebrews 10:35 NKJV).

Manifesting Desires

Ask or pray for the thing you desire—God knows what you need before you ask—and when you pray, be vigilant with thanksgiving (Colossians 4:2 NKJV). It is important to stay happy and positive.

Believe and receive (Mark 11:24 NKJV): "And whatsoever ye desire, believe that you have received it and you shall have it. Always remember it is God who works in you, both to will and do for His good pleasure."

When you believe, you act as though you are already driving your new car or living in your new house.

When you believe, you begin to feel excited, as though the car is in your garage or you are so happy to live in your dream house.

Forgive others (Mark 11:25 NKJV). It's a command to forgive if you want to receive your desires.

Read and meditate on scripture. Find a scripture that confirms the promise. For example, if you need healing, confess, "By His stripes I am healed" (Isaiah 53:5 NKJV).

Give thanks for what you have and what you are going to receive. It is already done. Be anxious for nothing, but by prayer and supplications, with thanksgiving, make your request known to God (Philippians 4:6 NKJV).

Show gratitude at all times through praise and worship. You shall worship the Lord your God only.

Turn your affection towards God and focus on His majestic power. He created the heavens and the earth (Genesis 1:1 NKJV).

Think of what you want all the time, and remain positive.

Think yourself happy throughout the day (Acts 26:2 NKJV).

Create a collage: keep pictures of the exact house, car, or holiday you want, or envision the size of your ministry. Visualise as often as you want throughout the day.

Be expectant—expect the things you want.

Visualise what it is you want, for example your new house or car.

God gives us clear instructions on how to take possession of a promise, in Acts 7:34 NKJV: He said, "I will send you to Egypt."

I believe that you must always be direct with God; you must ask or pray for your specific vision or dream to come true. Does your vision have an aspect of doing good for mankind? Is your vision going to have an impact on humanity? Are you willing to share and be a good steward of what God has given you? Your visions and dreams require faith. Sometimes you believe for something—let's say you desire to own a house in a specific area—but then you say, "I will take whatever the Lord gives me." It is important to focus on what you desire or have prayed for. You must not believe that it is a game of chance, like playing snakes and ladders, in which you accept the outcome wherever the dice may fall. If your request is very clear and specific, you must believe that God will bring it to pass.

Most of us know the story of the woman with the issue of blood. After she had spent all her money on physicians, she remained positive she would find a cure. One day someone told her about the miracle healings of Jesus. She believed in Him, and she started having a vision that if only she could touch the hem of His garment she would be healed.

She remained focused on her healing, while she waited for Jesus to come to her town. She already had a plan on how to take possession of her healing. Her vision was to go back to her family and live a normal life. You, too, can cultivate a habit of meditating on scripture day and night. Find a scripture that promises what you desire. For example, if you want a new house or car, meditate on this scripture: "And wherever the sole of your foot shall tread upon, that will I give unto you, as I said unto Moses" (Joshua 1:8 NKJV).

Faith in the Vision

A miracle is supernatural power. Once your vision is written down, call things forth as if they already exist. Faith does not come by knowledge but by revelation. Our knowledge must be turned into faith. Our Father can bring our dreams to pass today, tomorrow, or in a couple of months. We read in 2 Kings 7: 1 NKJV that Elisha said: "Thus said the Lord: 'Tomorrow at about this time a fine measure of flour will be sold for one shekel and two measures of barley for a shekel at the gates of Samaria.' We must act and take possession"; in 2 Kings 7:1 we read that God gives the promise to Elisha, and in verse 16 we see the promise came to pass.

Some time ago, I dreamed of a new car, I remember, and I decided to visit a showroom. On my second visit to the showroom, I walked around the car and then decided to claim this car by saying out loud the scripture. I opened each door and confessed the promise. At the last door, which was the front passenger door, I decided to just put my one foot in while meditating on Joshua 1:3 NKJV: "And wherever the sole of your foot shall tread upon, that will I give unto you as I said unto Moses."

When I took my foot away, I was stunned to see that the mark of my shoe was neatly imprinted on the mat. There was no way that my shoe print could remain just on the mat of the last door and not the rest of the car. I believed it was confirmation from God that my desire would come to pass. I continued to meditate on the word and took possession of this car ten months later in a very unusual way. We should continue to give praise, and thanksgiving should be continuously in our mouths. We receive by faith before we see and receive it in the natural.

We can start to trust God and see the invisible now, because Jesus promised us that "No eye has seen, no ear has heard, no mind has imagined what God can do for those who love Him (1 Corinthians 2:9 NKJV). When God blesses us, it's to glorify Him. When we have received our desires, we should give God all the glory. Let us remember the promise God gave to Habakkuk: "Even though it tarries, it will come."

It is important to enlarge your capacity to receive (Isaiah 54:2 NKJV); you must have big faith for big things and take the limits of God. We all start small, and as our faith grows, we desire bigger things. We can wrap ourselves in the promises of God, and we must see the visions first before we can take possession of them. When our visions are mixed with faith, God will intervene and provide by sending people into our lives to manifest whatever we need or want.

In the book of Genesis, we see that God called Abraham out of his tent at night to show him the stars. He gave him the vision and asked Abraham to have faith and believe that one day his descendants would be like the stars, too numerous to count.

All visions and dreams require a process. I remember sitting in a steam room with my drink bottle, which was filled with water. The cap of the bottle suddenly popped off. I was so surprised to see this happen; I later realised the pressure of the steam had caused the cap to pop off. At the time, a thought came to my mind that this is what happened when we prayed.

When we persist in prayer, the bottle gets fuller, and we get our answers from heaven; the Angels go to work on our behalf. I used this same example of the water bottle and filled it with faith; we know that faith grows exceedingly (2 Thessalonians 1:3 NKJV). Faith comes by hearing, and hearing by the Word of God, and if we continue to read the Bible, meditate on scripture, or listen to sermons, our faith grows. With hearing, our faith explodes, and the pressure is released by speaking out our faith. We continue to call things forth as if they exist already.

As we grow in faith, we desire to align ourselves with a vision of God. I used to picture Jesus, with a long, white robe, as in a picture I remembered from Sunday school. In all my visions and dreams, this is exactly how I see Jesus, but through revelation I now know that the image of Jesus is His character. He is love; He is kind, gentle, and faithful. To be fruitful, we must be obedient and use whatever is in our hands; we must use it for His kingdom. We need to stay connected to the Father, because we have to go through a process before we can receive manifestation.

It is important that we continue to remain positive, because nothing is impossible for God (Luke 1:37 NKJV). If God could open the prison doors for Peter, put a baby in Sarah's arms, open the Red Sea for Moses, and close the mouth of the lion for Daniel, then He can do anything for you. He rewards all those who honour Him and diligently seek Him.

When Jesus cursed the fig tree, the disciples heard it, but they did not see how the tree wasted away. It was not until their return that they noticed that the fig tree had withered away (Matthew 21:19 NKJV). The results could be the same with our prayers; sometimes we pray, feel, or see nothing. Sometimes we pray for healing; not all healing is immediate, but if we continue to believe in healing, breakthrough will come. We all received healing when Jesus died on the cross.

Life is not perfect; this is how life sometimes goes. There are times when our prayers or dreams come true, or there may be times when our dreams are on hold. Sometimes in life we will have to make sacrifices, and sometimes we will receive an abundance of blessings. At times we don't understand when things don't work out, but God has a bigger plan, even though we may not realise it at the time. He has promised that a vision is for an appointed time (Habakkuk 2:3 NKJV). Let us not misunderstand the place we are in—because God is aligning our lives for the next season.

Chapter 3

Faith—It's Voice Activated

My words to you are spirit and life (John 6:63 NKJV). "God says, 'My Spirit is upon thee, and My words, which I have put in thy mouth, shall not depart from thy mouth nor from the mouth of thy descendants or thy descendants' descendants,' says the Lord, 'from this time and forever more'" (Isaiah 59:21 NIV). The spoken word has power and will return to those who confess it. God said his Word would not return void. In the beginning God always said things (Genesis 1:3 NKJV). He said, "Let there be light." He spoke the earth into existence when He created the universe through calling it forth.

We should release our faith by speaking or saying it out loud. The Word of God is in our mouths, and Jesus is the high priest of our confession. We can clearly notice that everything is made up of what God has said. Speaking the Word is an act of faith, and faith is voice activated. We must say the same things as God does. And whatsoever we ask for in prayer, when we say it, we must believe that we have received it (Mark 11:23 NIV).

For our faith to grow, our minds have to hear the Word of God, so we can interpret it. We can listen to audio messages or sermons or read the Bible. His Word in our mouths, confessed by our lips, is powerful. Just imagine that if we can change our confession, we can change our lives. We can do this by guarding our hearts when we speak. The Bible says that the power of life and death is in the tongue (Proverbs 18:21 NIV). We can continually strive to offer the Lord the sacrifices of our praise, which is the fruit of our lips (Hebrews 13:15 NKJV); if we praise God throughout all seasons of our life, He is faithful, and he never changes. Jesus said in scripture that according to your faith it will be done for you.

What Is Faith?

Faith is a substance. Now, faith is the substance of things hoped for, the evidence of things not seen (Hebrews 11:1 NKJV). God gave faith to all of us, and He shows us how to use our faith. We have all been given a measure of faith. He is the author and finisher of our faith (Hebrews 12:2 NKJV). He told us to have faith in God (Mark 11:22 NKJV). We don't have to work for it; it's a free gift. Without faith, it is impossible to please God. Faith is in the *now*; it is already done. Our faith must be released towards God, and we must believe—because our faith unlocks the door to God's ability and power.

In the beginning was the Word, and the Word was with God, and the Word was God, and the Word was made flesh (John 1:1–4 NKJV). In the scripture *the Word* refers to Jesus. The Word, which is Jesus, was with God, and Jesus was God. We can see that Jesus was in the beginning with God, and through Jesus all things were made. In Him—Jesus—was life, and the life was the light of man.

God said, "Let us make man into our own image, after Our own likeness" (Genesis 1:20 NKJV). He was referring to the Trinity. The Trinity was from the beginning, and the Spirit of God hovered over the waters.

The Trinity: All Three as One.
God, the Father,
Jesus, the Son,
And the Holy Spirit.
All three existed since the beginning.

The Renewed Mind

The Bible tells us to set our minds or affections on things above. The Apostle Paul reminds us to put on, therefore, as the elect of God holy and beloved, tender mercies, kindness, humbleness of mind, meekness, and long-suffering. It is important to forgive one another and be forbearing towards one another. As believers, we must put on love, which is the bond of perfection, and we must let the peace of God rule in our hearts. He said, "Let the Word of Christ dwell in you richly in wisdom, teaching, and in admonishing one another in psalms and hymns and in spiritual songs, singing with grace in your heart to the Lord. Be mindful of whatever you do in deed or word; do it in the name of the Lord, and give thanks to God always" (Colossians 3:12–17 NIV).

Our minds are spiritual. If we can change our minds, we can change our lives. We read in the Bible that the prodigal son came to himself; he realised his father's servants were better off than he was. We have the ability to retrain our minds, and the Word of God renews our minds. We are all thinking beings, and it's important to speak out positive thoughts into the universe. We can all alter our future with our words—because our words start with our thoughts. We have the ability to change a thought we don't like as soon as we realise it. If we focus on happy and positive thoughts, it creates joy in our hearts.

Faith through Promise

The Bible is full of God's promises and all scriptures with a promise He will fulfil. Jesus is what He said He is, and He is no respecter of persons. He can do for you what He has done for all the great kings in the Bible. We receive His promises by faith. Faith is our title deed to ownership. When we show God our title deed—that is, our faith—He will evict the enemy off our property. We must believe that He is. Abraham believed God, and it was counted to him for righteousness (Genesis 4:3 NKJV). God's Word will not return void. The Bible is for our instruction, and we should start believing what we read in the Bible. Every answer to our problems is found in the Bible—for example, there are promises for your healing or your prosperity.

The Word of God effectively works in those who believe (1 Thessalonians 2:13 NKJV). God gives us the promise that it will be done for us according to our faith. The psalmist cries out to God, "Whom have I in heaven but you? And there is none upon earth that I desire beside you." If you belong to God, start acting, talking, and living as Jesus did when He was on earth.

Sometimes you may feel discouraged. Whatever you are feeling or going through, whatever season you are at in life, remember that the Bible always has something to say to you. It's the only book in which the advice is perfect for what you are going through. Scripture reminds us that for everything there is a season and a time to every purpose under heaven (Ecclesiastes 3:1 NIV). It is usually in the middle, when our faith grows, that God is quiet. He is busy working behind the scenes; don't get frustrated or discouraged, and keep the faith. If you feel anxious, depressed, sick, or fearful, you will find comfort in the Bible, if you follow its instructions. Jesus talks to us through His Word; we must be attentive to what we read and hear. Although the process may have been painful, God has done more in you than you realise. Take heart, because God is moving things around for you.

The Apostle Paul reminds us that our faith towards God has gone out, so that we do not need to say anything. Our actions demonstrate our faith, so that we do not need to say anything. Let your example do the talking. If we walk in faith, others can see without asking. If we look through scripture, the answer is guaranteed, and we have this promise in 2 Corinthians 9:10 NKJV: "Now may He who supplies the seed to the sower and bread for food also supply and multiply your store of seed." We must believe that, through faith, everything is already done.

We read in scripture how God instructed Moses to ask the king to let the Israelites go. When Moses realised that the promise of God was not taking place, he complained to God. He asked God, "Why did you send me here? Your people are mistreated since I did what you asked of me." Then the Lord replied to Moses, "Now you are going to see what I will do to the king. I will force him to let my people go" (Exodus 5:22–24 NKJV).

Sometimes we have a promise from God and it appears not to include all that He has promised. Moses cried out to God in a state of confusion, and sometimes this is what our Father wants; he wants us to talk to Him about our feelings, situations, and difficulties. Although God gives us instructions, He still wants us to call out to Him during the process of taking possession of the promise. It is important to be humble and to remain in the relationship with Him.

When God is at work in our lives or situations, sometimes it seems that things get harder or worse and nothing makes sense. It is during these times that we should cry out and ask God what is happening. It is often the big setbacks or trials that have the greatest provision. The Bible promises us that God gives us our heart's desire and does not withhold the request of our lips (Psalm 21:2 NKJV).

Faith Grows

We should have the same faith in Jesus; we can look at His life and His love for us when He was on earth. When we are born again, we belong to God. We should start to live, act, and talk as Jesus did. We have the promise that we are joint heirs in Christ (Romans 8:17 NKJV). It is written that the first man, Adam, became a living being, but the last Adam became a life-giving spirit. The first Adam came from the earth; the second Adam came from heaven (1 Corinthians 15:45 NIV).

If we have a relationship with Jesus, we grow daily in faith. We also grow in faith through prayer and worship. When we have faith, it explores what revelation reveals. Our faith must have action, because faith without works is dead (James 2:14 NKJV). Although faith is unseen, it only works with the invisible. Faith is not wishing that something will happen but trusting that whatever we believe in will come to pass. When our faith works with love, it can fix anything. God will do for us things that may seem impossible. When we read the story of the ten lepers, we see how Jesus sent them to show themselves to the priest. They were healed on the way, because they obeyed God.

Our faith can grow. We can read of Naaman, the leper who was a wealthy man. When he was told to wash in the Jordan seven times, he turned away angrily. After his servant spoke with him, he agreed to go and dip in the Jordan (2 Kings 5 NKJV). This man got faith on the way; his faith grew exceedingly, and he was healed (2 Thessalonians

1:2 NKJV). We can grow our faith by listening to audio sermons or by reading the Bible. In most cases we can grow our faith by listening to the testimonies of other people. Their breakthroughs can stir up our faith; we realise that if God can do something for them, then we can expect Him to do the same for us.

How Do We Get Faith?

Faith comes when we hear, and hearing comes by the Word of God (Romans 10:17 NKJV). We must read the Bible every day, even a few minutes a day, to stay connected to God. When we read the Bible, we see that God is revealing Jesus to us. Jesus said, "Take heed of what you hear; with the same measure you use it, it will be measured back to you." We grow daily into believing, as we hear and meditate on the Word of God. We get faith by seeking the presence of God every day. When we see changes in other believers and see how blessed they are, we are inspired, and we desire to remain in relationship with Jesus.

Our Faith Can Move Mountains: Mark 5:36 NKJV, and You Must Speak To Your Mountain: Mark 11:23–25 NKJV

If we lack finances, we should speak directly to this. Say, "Financial lack be removed."

"I pull you out by the roots and I cast you into the sea."

Do not doubt in your heart.

Amelia Nazer

Believe what you say, and it will be done.

Forgive when you pray, so that your sins may be forgiven.

God has given us power and authority to speak to the mountain.

As we grow in faith, we realise that we must believe that whatever we have asked, we have received it in Jesus's name.

Blessings through Faith

We receive everything from God through faith. We must first receive from God before we can give. Adam received from God; he was given a garden, and all he had to do was dress it (Genesis2:15 NKJV). Faith will bring us to a new place where we are able to operate at God's level. As we grow in Christ, we grow from faith to faith. We don't live in the past; each new day brings new hope. God's mercy is new every day.

Faith needs action, and sometimes we need to encourage ourselves by saying, in faith, that God is taking us from survival mode to oversupply, to be a source or blessings for many. We should not have selfish ambition but always try to be good stewards over what God has allocated or blessed us with.

In Luke 7:6 NKJV we see a centurion who sends friends to say to Jesus, "Lord, don't trouble yourself, but just say the word, and my servant will be healed." He had bold faith when he believed that his servant would be healed. We see throughout scripture that Jesus always spoke with power and authority. We are encouraged to do the same in our everyday lives. Our faith can move mountains. Jesus said, "Don't be afraid, only believe" (Mark 5:36 NKJV).

Faith is what connects us to God's righteousness. Faith is speaking to our problems, and we must speak positive things about ourselves. Our words start with thoughts. God told Joshua, "If you want good success, meditate on the word day and night (Joshua 1:8 NKJV). Sometimes we need to ask ourselves, "What am I thinking about? Is it thoughts that will build me up or thoughts that interfere with what God wants to be for me? What do I focus on?" Can you see the impossible now? As a man thinks in his heart, so is he (Proverbs23:7 NKJV). Faith means receiving the impossible now. We must call things forth as if they exist; for example, we can say, "By His stripes I am healed" or "I am debt free."

Our hearts and mouths are connected, and our faith is voice activated. We must speak out our faith. We can meditate on the Word of God by saying it out loud. The more we say it, the more our hearts will store it. Our mouths will speak what our hearts are full of. We can speak blessings over ourselves and others; for example, we can bless our family or friends: "The Lord bless thee and keep thee; The Lord makes His face shine upon thee."

Faith and Spiritual Power

When we have faith, we use the power given to us by Jesus to overcome enemies. We become spiritual warriors. Satan cannot interfere with the Word, but he can tamper with our minds and feelings. The enemy is very good; he knows how to distract us and make us feel discouraged. When we grow in faith, Satan will attack our minds, but if we remain steadfast in our faith, we can bind our enemies. We have the keys to the kingdom, because whatever we bind on earth is bound in heaven, and whatever we loose on earth is loosed in heaven (Matthew 18:18; Matthew 16:19 NKJV).

Sometimes we get frustrated with family and friends, when things don't go our way. When this happens, it's a good time to channel all this energy against our enemies. When we are under attack, we should get angry with the enemy; we should rise up and take authority. We can tell the enemy who is in charge; we can make it clear that *we* are in charge when we are in spiritual warfare. Our enemies will always try to break the rhythm of our power by bringing obstacles into the relationship. We have been given the power to tread over serpents; it is our promise from God.

Many times, when we become discouraged or things get difficult, we fight God, but we should rather fight our position *in* God. The Apostle Paul reminds us to put on the shield of faith (Ephesians 6:8–10 NIV). We see from the full armour of God that the shield which is faith allows us to quench all the fiery darts of the wicked. The shield of faith can cover all the vital organs of the body, and with the shield we must be vigilant to protect ourselves from our enemies. We must pick up our shields and fight the good fight, confront the enemy, and claim what is ours. With our shields of faith, we can face the enemy with confidence. We are in spiritual warfare at all times, and faith allows us to press on and gives us victory.

Ask yourself, "How big is my faith? Am I covered by the shield of faith?" Faith covers all so that we may lack nothing. We are children of the Most High, and we receive by faith what Jesus has already done. He died on the cross for our sins; we received forgiveness and healing. By His stripes we are healed.

Faith through Trust

When we have faith, we always look at what God is doing in our lives, not what he is *not* doing. We must trust that those who believe in Him shall have everlasting life (John: 3:16 NKJV).

It is important to have the correct image of God—not the physical portrait we see on Christmas cards but the image of His character. He is love, peace, and joy, and He is faithful. Once we have the correct image of God, we will strive to become obedient and will enjoy our blessings by faith. "O, taste and see that the Lord is good" (Psalm 34:8 NIV). Although we are joint heirs with Christ, we must step up to take that privilege by being holy as He is Holy. To be a joint heir means that we must have the same character as Christ.

The fruit of the Spirit is love, joy, peace, kindness, goodness, long-suffering, and faithfulness (Galatians 5:22 NIV).

When we face obstacles or difficulties, we must use our faith by speaking to the mountain. Our faith will bring whatever we desire to pass. Faith is not hoping for an answer, but it is knowing that it is already done. When we trust God, He will fight our battles. He invites us to cast our cares and leave all our troubles or worries at His feet. It is important to surrender complete trust; we must not doubt that God will help us.

Some time ago I had a dream; in this dream I was in heaven. I saw my best friend, Bridget, and she was very happy and content. I was unhappy to be in heaven and told her that I had asked God for long life. While I was still complaining to her, people started walking around us, and before I knew it, I found myself being carried on a man's back. I tried to look at his face, but he just kept spinning around so that I could not see his face. After a few attempts at trying to figure out who this was, I just surrendered, and all of a sudden I leaned over his shoulder and whispered in his ear, "I love You Lord."

He whispered back, "I love you too." As soon as I let go and trusted the person, the answer came. Faith sometimes is like that. You don't have to figure out everything, just believe—let go and let God. To have faith is to trust even when you cannot see any solution to your problem.

Faith Must Have Action

Some of us have read about Bartholomew, the blind man who wanted to receive his sight. He was sitting by the roadside and called out, "Jesus, Son of David, have mercy on me." He showed his faith by taking off his garment and running to Jesus. He was desperate to be healed.

Jesus asked him, "What do you want me to do for you?"

The blind man said, "Rabbi, I want to see."

"Go," said Jesus, "Your faith has healed you" (Mark 10:46–52 NIV). This blind man took a chance on Jesus; he called out for his healing. What are you going to do with your situation? Faith without works is dead (James 2:26 NKJV).

We read throughout the Bible that when people were desperate for healing they acted on their faith. A man who was not able to move was lowered through the roof to receive his healing. His friends acted on his behalf; they had fierce faith that this man would be healed (Luke 5:18 NKJV).

We read in scripture that God asked Ezekiel to speak to the dry bones. Although Ezekiel had doubt at first, he obeyed and prophesied to the dry bones and saw them come to life. Ezekiel had to speak out his faith (Ezekiel 37:3–10 NKJV).

Faith with action means we mix faith with the Word of God; we believe and meditate on scripture until we receive the promise. Moses released his faith towards God by raising his rod to part the Red Sea. We can release our faith towards God by speaking it out, and we must believe God in order to receive His promises from the Bible.

Chapter 4

The Holy Spirit

Jesus said, "I will pour out My Spirit on all flesh, and your sons and daughters will prophesy, your old men will dream dreams, and young men will see visions" (Joel 2:28 NIV).

"You will receive power when the Holy Spirit comes upon you" (Act 1:8 NIV).

God sends out His Spirit to any place to accomplish His will, and He renews the face of the earth (Psalm 104:30 NIV).

I grew up learning about Jesus, but the Holy Spirit was not often preached about in church. I will just briefly explain who the Holy Spirit is and what the Holy Spirit wants to be for us. We cannot be in touch with the Father and the Son without the Holy Spirit (Ephesians 2:18 NKJV). The Holy Spirit is part of the Trinity: the Father, the Son, and the Holy Spirit.

Who Is the Holy Spirit?

The Holy Spirit is God's power in action in our lives (Micah 3:8 NKJV). He is a person; He has feelings; He has a will and can speak. He is the third person of the Trinity. He is equal to God; they are all One.

Jesus said, "I will send you a Helper and a Comforter; it is better that I go away." (John 14:26 NKJV) Our helper is the Holy Spirit.

The Bible refers to the Holy Spirit as God's hands or fingers (Psalm 8:3 NKJV). Just as a craftsman uses hands and fingers to do his work, God has used His Spirit to create the universe.

The Holy Spirit is the power of God that works in us, and He reveals to us Jesus Christ (Ephesians 3:20 NKJV).

What Does the Holy Spirit Do?

He is our helper and teacher.

He gives us wisdom, if we ask.

He comforts, guides, and protects us.

He convinces us to change our behaviour or prompts us to do the right thing. He knows our entire beings; we don't have to explain our behaviour or mistakes to Him, because He knows our weaknesses.

He eagerly waits for us to ask things from Him.

He longs for us to acknowledge Him, by talking to Him every day.

He wants to be our best friend, if we acknowledge Him through all seasons of life.

The Holy Spirit gives us many gifts for the honour and glory of God.

He prays the perfect will of God, when we pray in the spirit or tongues.

Why Is the Holy Spirit Given to Us?

The Holy Spirit is a free gift to us from God.

He knows the gift that is stored in us and will instruct us.

The Holy Spirit teaches and guides us into all truth.

He gives us utterance to pray in the spirit; we pray the perfect will of God (Acts: 2:4 NKJV). When we pray in the spirit, or other tongues, the devil does not know what we are praying.

The Holy Spirit is given to us to invest in others; God wants to work through us.

God uses the example of wind to describe the Holy Spirit: and the wind blows where it wants, and you hear the sound of it but cannot tell where it comes from, so is anyone who is born of the spirit (John 3:8 NKJV).

How Is the Power of the Holy Spirit Working in Us?

When we continue to pray and ask for guidance and help.

We stir up the gift when we are always thinking about God.

It gives us an opportunity to always think on good things that are true, noble, and just.

We should acknowledge the Holy Spirit throughout each day and continue to meditate on the Word.

If we continuously pray in the Spirit, we pray the Will of the Father and become refreshed. We are prompted by the Holy Spirit to pray the will of the Father for ourselves and others.

The Word of God is spirit; we must worship Him in spirit and in truth (John 4:24 NKJV). We are spirit beings, and we have the same spiritual quality as Jesus does. The Holy Spirit wants to operate through us, but He needs our hands, feet, and mouths.

My spirit knows all about me; it is one with God. We are all spiritual beings in bodies of flesh. Our spirits are always willing, but our flesh is weak. When we walk in the Spirit, we shall not fulfil the lust of the flesh; therefore if we live in the spirit, we must also walk in the spirit. To walk in the spirit is to walk in love, joy, and peace. It is to be kind, loving, and forgiving. If we walk in the spirit, we crucify our flesh, because our flesh rules our emotions through bad habits. The Holy Spirit helps us to stay in covenant with God, and all we need to do is to trust Him. Scripture reminds us to be renewed in the spirit of our minds (Ephesians 4:23 NKJV).

Where Does the Holy Spirit Live?

He lives inside of us when we are born again.

He walks besides us. He will never leave us.

He is to us what Jesus was to His disciples.

The Holy Spirit empowers us and gives us strength to do all things.

He rests upon us and He dwells on the earth.

When Do We Receive the Holy Spirit?

When we are born again, He breathed on them and said receive the Holy Spirit.

When each one of us, confesses that Jesus is our Lord and Saviour (Romans10:9 NKJV).

We receive power when we receive the Holy Spirit.

The baptism of the Holy Spirit is different to being filled with the Holy Spirit. I will not discuss the baptism here.

The Fruits of the Holy Spirit

These fruits are love, joy, peace, kindness, goodness, longsuffering, faithfulness, self-control, and goodness (Galatians 5:22 NKJV).

All scripture regarding the names, attributes, symbols, sins, and power of the Holy Spirit is taken from the New King James Version.

The Holy Spirit has many names in the Bible. He is known as

1. God: Acts 5:3–4
2. Lord: 2 Corinthians 3:18
3. Spirit: 1 Corinthians 2:10
4. Spirit of God: 1 Corinthians 3:16
5. Spirit of truth: John 15:26
6. Eternal Spirit: Hebrews 9:14

Attributes or characteristics of the Holy Spirit. He is

1. Loving: Romans 15:30
2. Omnipotent: Luke 1:35
3. Omnipresent: Psalm 139:7–10
4. Having a will
5. Eternal: Hebrews 9:14
6. Able to speak: Acts 8:29, Acts 13:2

Symbols of Holy Spirit

1. Dove: Matthew 3:16
2. Wind: Acts 2: 1–4
3. Fire: Acts 2:3

Sins against the Holy Spirit

1. Blasphemy: Matthew 12:31
2. Resistance, unbelief: Acts 7:57
3. Insult: Hebrews 10:29
4. Lies: Acts 5:3
5. Grief: Ephesians 4:30
6. Quenching of the Spirit: 1 Thessalonians 5:19

Power in Christ

1. Conceived of: Matthew 1:18–20
2. Baptism: Matthew 3:16
3. Led by: Luke 4:1
4. Filled with power: Luke 4:14–16
5. Witness of Jesus: John 15:26
6. The power that raised Jesus from the dead: Romans: 8:11

The Holy Spirit

We have the privilege to ask our Helper anything, and He is willing and waiting to serve our every need. We should cultivate a habit of talking to the Holy Spirit every day, because the Spirit of God yearns jealously (James 4:5 NKJV).

I am sure many of you have heard or sung the hymn "Be Still and Know that I Am God." Not so long ago I was humming this hymn while driving. The song just came to me, as it had in the past, so I asked the Holy Spirit what it meant, what message was in it for me. Within minutes I got the revelation: "Be conscious of the power in you. Think of this power all the time." It made complete sense, because when you are still and thinking of God, you become conscious of who He is and that He lives in you. You become aware that He can, and wants to, give you everything, if you let Him. This power wants to talk to you, if you are willing to listen.

It is important that we acknowledge His presence, because He lives in us. Just imagine how a friend would feel if you were to meet for coffee and for the entire hour or so you didn't say a word to him or her. We have an opportunity each day to discuss our plans with our Helper. The Holy Spirit wants to work through us. He needs our hands, feet, and mouths. He helps us to become Christlike by convincing us to change our habits or do the right thing. For example, we may have a desire to start tithing. When we receive the Holy Spirit, it is as Jesus said to his disciples: "Greater things than these will you do." We have all received spiritual gifts from above. Jesus performed His miracles by the power of the Holy Spirit. Jesus gave us power and authority to have dominion over the earth.

When I got the revelation to talk to the Holy Spirit every day, it took effort and commitment to acknowledge the

Holy Spirit. I had to learn and practise to continue to speak to Him throughout the day, to cultivate a habit to ask and tell Him everything. Just imagine receiving a birthday or Christmas gift that you eagerly unwrap to see what is inside. We need the same excitement and anticipation to see what the Holy Spirit has in store for us each day. It should be a delight to spend time with God. When I wake up each morning, the first thing I say is, "Good morning, Holy Spirit." He is a person. Ask Him what He would like you to do for the day. Always ask to be a blessing to someone you will meet during the course of the day.

Our busy and sometimes stressful lifestyles demand a lot of our time, but we can talk to the Holy Spirit while we are cleaning the house, driving, or even playing with the kids. The anointing is within us; we don't have to go anywhere to acknowledge His presence (1 John 2:27 NKJV).

The Holy Spirit wants to be our best friend, but He leaves the choice with us. We all have a free will to engage or seek Him. When we see the Holy Spirit with our spiritual eyes, we realise that He is not a coat that we put on and take off every day. The Holy Spirit wants to walk with us at all times, regardless of the season we are in.

Our feelings have nothing to do with the presence of the Holy Spirit. Some days we may feel consumed or overwhelmed by His presence, and at other times we may feel emptiness. Feelings are not always true, and the way we feel is not an indication of whether He is absent; we must not rely on feelings. As I was growing in my spiritual journey, I realised how important it was to pray in the Spirit.

The Holy Spirit is like a small, still voice; He prompts us gently to yield to Him. I remember that, years ago, I had a desire to volunteer in church, but I kept making excuses, with my busy work schedule, which included working on weekends. A recurrent thought, especially if it is biblical— for example, fasting or tithing—will not go away if the Holy Spirit is convincing you. He guides and gives you the ability to do what is right.

All good desires are from God, and the Holy Spirit will bring it to pass; all we need to do is to believe and receive it. Many times He talks to us through pictures, people, and songs. It is important to test these and see if they lines up with scripture or the nature of God.

I had a vision of Jesus standing at my bedside. His white robe had shades of blue, green, and scarlet, and He said these words to me twice: "I will never leave you." I woke up wondering whether something bad was going to happen. Jesus promised never to leave us (Deuteronomy: 31:6 NIV) when He was on earth. He was bombarded by people requesting healing and deliverance.

We are very fortunate today to have the Holy Spirit in us. I had trouble in the beginning, being persistent, in acknowledging the Holy Spirit, but it becomes second nature if you pray in the Spirit every day. These days more people get baptised by water, and the church speaks more about the presence of the Holy Spirit. It is becoming evident that churches are hungry for revival and need the presence of the Holy Spirit, especially now as we are living in end times.

We are spirit beings, and we are made to receive spiritual gifts. We must always be in a position of prayer; we must be still and listen to hear God's voice. The Word of God has the power to fulfil itself. We read in Genesis 3 what God came to accomplish on earth.

When Adam and Eve fell, they lost their source, the Spirit of God to them, in them, and through them. They lost their foundation, which was the source of life. Jesus came so that we might have life and life abundantly (John 10:10 NKJV).

We have the promise of God's power, that God is able to do exceedingly, abundantly, above all, according to His power that works in us (Ephesians 3:20 NKJV). The power of God is expressed to us from Him, and it will allow us to change the way we see things. Jesus said, "You will receive rivers of living waters," which I believe is the Holy Spirit. In the Old Testament, God appeared to men and prophets in visions and dreams; sometimes angels did too. We can see, however, in the New Testament, that Jesus went away and gave us a greater gift, the Holy Spirit, which is eagerly waiting to serve our every need. We are blessed in the fact that we don't need to queue or walk from city to city to get a glimpse of Jesus. He lives in us; all we need to do is enter into His presence and call on His name. We have already received the gift of healing; by His stripes we are healed. We don't have to be like the woman with the issue of blood who was desperate to touch His garment to receive her healing.

The Holy Spirit comes into agreement with God; He prompts us to make good decisions, and He directs our steps. God's home is in us. Our bodies are His temples, and the Holy Spirit lives in these temples.

The Holy Spirit is just as much God as are the Father and the Son. I recently had a vision or dream myself and a group of people walking along a road, it looked like a road out of the Old Testament. A group of people were walking far ahead; they were already at a bend in the road but were still in sight. A few of us were walking behind Jesus, who was on my right. I was drinking tea from a white polystyrene cup. I walked up to Jesus and offered Him some of my tea. He said to me, "I must first ask My Father if I can take the cup from you."

Then, from the left of the crowd, I saw God walking towards Jesus. They looked identical, wearing the same white robes, but I could not see God's face. He walked over to Jesus, kissed Him on the lips, and said, "You may take the cup from her."

Then Jesus turned to me and said, "I've wanted to take this cup from you for a long time." He was smiling happily. I woke up, but I did not understand this dream until a few months later.

One day during my devotional time, while I was reading the Bible, the words "cast your cares" felt like it was jumping out of the page and reminded me of my dream a few months ago and my perception of "cast your cares on Him" took on a different perspective. I've had a few visions or dreams from God, and most of them seem to encourage me. I have decided that, despite my seasons of life, nothing will prevent me from serving God. The Bible promised that we are all blessed coming in and blessed going out (Deuteronomy 28:6). God is good all the time; we need to seek His Face, and He will have communion with us.

The Works of the Holy Spirit

All Bible scripture is taken from the New International Version (NIV)

He gives us access to God: Ephesians 2:8
He anoints us for service: Luke 4:18
He assures us that we are God's children: Romans 8:15–16, Galatians 4:6
He baptises us: John 1:26
He calls and commissions us: Acts 13:24, Acts 20:28
He convicts us of sin: John 16:9
He creates: Genesis 1:2
He empowers believers: 1 Thessalonians 1:5, Luke 24:47
He gives us spiritual gifts: 1 Corinthians 12:8–11
He helps us in our weakness: Romans 8:28
He dwells in believers: Romans 8:9
He interprets scripture: 1 Corinthians 2:1
He moulds our character: Galatians 5:22–23
He sanctifies us: Romans 5:8
He seals us: Ephesians 1:13–14
He strengthens us: Ephesians 3:16
He teaches: John 14:26
He testifies of Jesus: John 15:26
He gives us victory over flesh: Romans 8:2–4

Jesus said that the Holy Spirit will teach us all things and bring to our remembrance all that He said (John 14:26 NKJV). A primary role of the Holy Spirit is that He bears witness of Jesus Christ and He talks to people's hearts about the truth of Jesus Christ.

In the beginning I found it easier to pray in the spirit/tongues than to talk to Him as I would a friend. It is important to realise that the Holy Spirit is a person, and He yearns to be in relationship with us. We must picture the Holy Spirit as peace and love and yearn to remain in His presence. In the Old Testament, people had visions and dreams from God or angels, but in the New Testament we have the Holy Spirit living in us.

When a person becomes born again by confessing and believing and receiving Jesus Christ, God resides in that person through the Holy Spirit, and that person's body is a temple of God (1 Corinthians 3:16 NIV).

Chapter 5

God's Love

For God so loved the world that He gave His only begotten Son, that whoever believes in Him shall not perish but have everlasting life (John 3:16 NKJV). God's love never fails. As humans, we all have the basic need to love and be loved. We all receive God's love when we receive Jesus as our Lord and Saviour. Jesus said, "I command you to love each other as much as I love you." God demonstrates His love through His many promises in the Bible.

For unto us a child is born, unto us a Son is given, and He will be called Wonderful, Counsellor, Mighty God, Everlasting Father, Prince of Peace (Isaiah 9:6 NIV).

Jesus was truly human and truly divine. He walked on the earth as a man, He ate food, slept, and did all things that we human beings do. He was tempted by Satan, just as we are tempted by him today. God loved us so much that He sent His only son to die on the cross for our sins and to give us victory over the enemy. The Father's love allowed Jesus to feed the hungry, heal the sick, and cast out demons.

God gives us His love to love others, and we can love others by faith. When we love our neighbours, with God's love, we can change the world. This kind of love allows us to forgive those who have hurt, frustrated, or angered us. Many times it's hard to love those who are difficult, but we can love them by faith.

We know that God loves us just the way we are. The Apostle Paul said that apart from love, anything we might do for God or others is of no value. All we do must be motivated by God's love (1 Corinthians 13 NIV).

In the Old Testament, Isaiah prophesied about Jesus the Messiah who God sent to save mankind.

The Messiah as Prophesied by Isaiah

Scripture is from the New King James Version

He will be born of a virgin: Isaiah 7:14
He will be heir to the throne of David: Isaiah 9:6–7
He will have His way prepared: Isaiah 40:3–4
He will be exalted: Isaiah 52:13
He will make blood atonement: Isaiah 53:5
He will be widely rejected: Isaiah 53:6–8
He will voluntarily accept our punishment: Isaiah 53:7–8
The Gentiles will seek Him: Isaiah 11:10
He will be silent before His executors: Isaiah 53:7
He will be buried in a rich man's tomb: Isaiah 53:9
He will save those who believe in Him: Isaiah 53:12

Prophesy of Isaiah Fulfilled: Jesus the Messiah
Scripture is from the New King James Version

He was born of a virgin, Mary: Luke 1:26–31
He was given the throne of His father, David: Luke 1:32–33
He was announced by John the Baptist: Luke 1:76
He was highly exalted by God and the people: Philippians 2:10
He shed His blood to atone for our sins:
He was not accepted by many: John 15:25
He took our sins: John 1:29
The Gentiles came to speak to Jesus: John 12:20
He was silent before Herod: Luke 23:9
He was buried in Joseph's tomb: Mark 15:46
He provided salvation for all who believe: John 3:16, Acts 16:31

When Jesus was ready to start His ministry, He was given the book of the prophet Isaiah, and when He had opened the book, He found the place where it is written, "The Spirit of the Lord is upon Me, because He has anointed me to preach the gospel to the poor; He has sent Me to heal the broken-hearted, to proclaim liberty to the captives and recovery of sight to the blind, to set at liberty those who are oppressed; to proclaim the acceptable year of the Lord." Then He closed the book. And He said, "Today this Scripture is fulfilled in your hearing (Luke 4:17 NIV). Jesus revealed to them that He was the Messiah when He read the Scriptures to them.

Again the high priest asked him, "Are you the Messiah, the Son of the Blessed One?"

"I am," said Jesus (Mark 14:61–62).

The Names of God

Wonderful

1. He loves us and is kind at all times.
2. He is our provider.
3. We are fearfully and wonderfully made.
4. He wrote His new covenant in our hearts.
5. His Word will never return void.
6. He never changes; He is the same today, yesterday, and forever.

The Mighty God

1. He can do all things.
2. Nothing is impossible for Him.
3. He created the heavens and the earth.
4. He called things into existence.
5. He protects and directs our paths.
6. He anoints us and gives us His Holy Spirit.

Prince of Peace

1. He is peace and love.
2. He governs the earth with His love.
3. He is a peacemaker.
4. He gives us peace beyond our understanding.
5. He said, "My peace I give you, not as the world gives you."

Everlasting Father

1. He is the alpha and the omega.
2. His Word will never cease.
3. He is the Father of lights.
4. We are His chosen people.
5. He went to prepare a place for us.
6. He gave us dominion over the earth.

Counsellor

1. We can talk to God at any time we want.
2. He is timeless and ever-present in our time of need.
3. He encourages us to ask for all our needs.
4. The government rests on His shoulders.
5. His love is infinite.
6. He became man for our sake, and we can ask Him anything.

God Is Love

God's love is and will always be unconditional. There is nothing we have to do to earn His love. The first two commandments are our greatest, and the first is that we must love the Lord our God with all our hearts, minds, and souls. The second commandment is to love our neighbours as ourselves. The Apostle Paul reminds us: above all, love each other deeply, because love covers all (1 Peter 4:8 NKJV).

God gives us the ability to love others; He pours His love into our hearts, and His love is immeasurable and infinite.

His love is from eternity to eternity, and He reveals His secrets to those who love Him (Psalm 103:17 NKJV).

When we have God's love, we experience inner peace. This love is given to us by God, and it is compassionate; we won't have the desire to steal, kill, or commit adultery. If we have the love of God in us, we will freely give to others; we will share and help to eradicate poverty, crime, and violence completely. When we love others, we have a desire to give more of ourselves, and we experience joy when we express love to each other. We also have the assurance that we don't owe anything to man except to love him (Romans 13:8 NKJV). Our love for God gives us a desire to always praise and worship Him.

God loves us so much that he gave us His power to work in us. The promise is in Ephesians 3:20 (NIV) "Now to him who is able to do immeasurably more than all we ask or imagine, according to his power that is at work within us." God's power is at work in us when we walk in love, when we choose to forgive others. The Father works through us when we remain humble and bow before Him with open hearts. Our love is demonstrated when we serve others and put their needs before our own. Our Father is able to do far more for us than we could ever think or imagine; He is not limited by our circumstances or situations.

The fruit of the Spirit is love, and our love grows every day. Paul writes, "May the Lord make your love increase and overflow for each other and for everyone else" (1 Thessalonians 3:12 NIV). When we love others God's way, we start to see them as God sees them.

We are reminded of what love is: it is patient, kind, never jealous or envious; it's never boastful or proud, never selfish or rude. Love does not demand its own way, and it is not irritable. It does not even notice when others do wrong; love goes on forever, and it never fails. There are three things that remain: faith, hope, and love; the greatest of these is love (1 Corinthians 13 NIV).

I remember one morning when I woke up with an overwhelming feeling of love. I felt an inner peace and joy. I knew then that God had downloaded his love to me, to love others just as He loved me. My attitude changed, and it made clear sense that preachers would tell their congregation that they loved them. They could love anyone, because it was God's love in them; He gave them the ability to love others. It is very easy to love anyone with God's love, because He *is* love. It is important to declare your love to God.

When we have a relationship with God, we experience his unique love for us. This love is not based on our performance, and there is nothing we can do to cause Him to love us any more or less than He already does. God's Word says to make love your highest aim.

The character of God, His wonderful works and promises, and His love for His people are demonstrated in Psalm 111 (NKJV).

Praise the Lord

1. I will praise the Lord with my whole heart, in the assembly of the upright and in the congregation.
2. The works of the Lord are great, studied by all who have pleasure in them.
3. His work is honourable and glorious, and His righteousness endures forever.
4. He has made His wonderful works to be remembered: The Lord is gracious and full of compassion.
5. He has given food to those who fear Him; He will ever be mindful of His covenant.
6. He has declared to His people the power of His works, In giving them the heritage of the nations.
7. The works of His hands are verity and justice; All His precepts are sure.
8. They stand fast forever and ever, And are done in truth and uprightness.
9. He has sent redemption to His people, He has commanded His covenant forever. Holy and awesome is His name.
10. The fear of the Lord is the beginning of wisdom; A good understanding have all who do His commandments. His praise endures forever.

Chapter 6

Gratitude

Gratitude is defined as the quality of being thankful, the readiness to show appreciation for something and return kindness.

It is a state of being thankful. To feel grateful is to feel thankful for something or someone. Gratitude is a feeling of thankfulness, and it has an element of love in it.

Jesus taught us the importance of giving thanks to the Father by example. When He gave thanks to the Father, He lifted up His eyes and said, "Father, I thank you that you have heard me." We all realise that God created man to honour Him by giving Him thanks. As believers, we acknowledge that He is our king, and we maintain an attitude of gratitude for what He has done for us on earth.

When Jesus was on earth, He always gave thanks before an event. When he broke the few fish and seven loaves of bread, he gave thanks first, and then he gave the food to his disciples to share (Matthew 15:36 NKJV).

Another example of Jesus giving thanks is, "He took the cup, and when he had given thanks, he said: 'Take this and divide it among yourselves.'" (Luke 22:17 NKJV).

It is important to always be grateful towards the Creator. The Apostle Paul reminds us to have an attitude of gratitude and to be joyful and thankful (Colossians 1:12 NKJV). We are commanded to give thanks always and for everything to God the Father, in the name of our Lord, Jesus Christ (Ephesians 5:20 NKJV). Our thankfulness should be displayed in our everyday life, because thankful people are always full of joy. We always tell God that we are thankful for all we have received or are going to receive. When we give thanks, we do the will of God. As believers, we are reminded to give thanks to God in all circumstances, for this is the will of God in Christ Jesus for us (1 Thessalonians 5:18 NKJV).

When we are in a relationship and have fellowship with Jesus, thanksgiving becomes our priority each morning as soon as we wake up. We give thanks to the Lord for a new day and another chance to serve Him. David encouraged us to make a joyful noise unto the Lord; he always thanked God for any season in his life (Psalm 100:1–2 NKJV). Gratitude always flows from the heart; it is an attitude that comes out of our habit of giving thanks.

It is important to always express our thankfulness towards others. The Bible instructs us to encourage one another at all times; therefore, we should encourage one another and build one another up (1 Thessalonians 5:14 NKJV). We can choose to say positive and uplifting things to each other, and by complimenting others, we may change their circumstances. Many times we have met people and given them a word of encouragement; they will sometimes confess that our encouragement has allowed them to change their minds about something. For example, someone may have been considering divorcing a spouse. To encourage others can also save their lives, as they may decide to stop their destructive lifestyles.

In the Old Testament; the Egyptian army pursued Moses and the Israelites as they headed towards the Red Sea. They were in trouble, but once they were safe, the Israelites praised God for protecting them from the enemy by drying up the Red Sea (Exodus 15:1–19 NKJV). They expressed their gratitude through praise and worship. When you have prayed to the Father, give thanks while you are waiting for the promise to manifest.

We read in the Bible that when Daniel was in trouble he said, "I thank thee and praise thee, O thou God of my fathers." Then God revealed the secrets to Daniel to interpret the dream of King Nebuchadnezzar.

As believers, we desire to give God our praise and thanks, because we are instructed to let the peace of God rule in our hearts, to which we are called, and be thankful (Colossians 3:15 NKJV). We experience joy when we are thankful, and it generates a feeling of wellbeing.

It is important to think about simple things each day to thank God for. God is the giver of good things, and all good things come from above (James 1:17 NKJV).

Everyday Blessings to Give Him Thanks throughout the Day

1. You can give thanks for a new day.
2. Give thanks for your family.
3. Think of all the appliances in your kitchen that make life easy: for example, an electric kettle to boil water for your morning coffee.
4. What about the continuous hot water in the house to shower or bathe whenever we want, which we so easily take for granted?
5. Give thanks for your job, which provides an income.
6. Envisage friends whom you can visit or contact.
7. Be grateful for the abundance of food in your cupboards.
8. Be thankful for the clothes you have.
9. Picture the house you live in, the roof over your head to protect you.
10. Give thanks for your car, if you own one, or for the convenience of public transport.

Our gratitude is expressed when thankfulness becomes a way of life. It flows from our hearts and mouths, because we are genuinely thankful. We recognise that Jesus died on the cross for our sins; if we have received the revelation of the cross, we have changed our mind set. We realise that

His blood covers it all, and we have received our healing by His stripes. When we are fully aware of His greatness, we humbly give him praise and thanks all throughout the day. When we are in a state of thankfulness, our focus moves away from our selfish desires, and we realise that God is in control. When we are thankful, we know we belong to God, because he has blessed us. Our thankfulness towards God allows us to experience an abundant life (John 10:10 NKJV).

I have realised that when you shift your thinking to have a posture or attitude of gratitude, the universe opens up to you. I am sure many of you have heard pastors preach about using your faith to believe for simple things like a parking spot. From experience, I know it works, but I have now adopted an attitude of giving thanks for the parking spot as soon as I enter the car park. In 98 per cent of cases I have found it without effort, and I will continue my thanksgiving for unseen things.

I have cultivated a habit of thanksgiving and expressing gratitude even though I have not seen any breakthrough. We should always give thanks with a smile; when it comes from the heart, we will experience joy. When our thanks start to overflow, the universe brings back much more than we could anticipate. I always remind myself how good our Creator is, and I thank Him out loud for his goodness. I always pray this: "Thank you, Lord, that I am alive to see yet another day. Show me who I can be a blessing to. I thank you, Lord, for who I am in you and who I am becoming."

In a recent dream I found myself in a beautiful garden. It was obvious that it must have rained, because the raindrops were still visible on the leaves. The greenery in the garden was amazing. I saw a dash of sunshine coming through the entrance. The garden was perfect; I have never seen anything like it. As I was admiring the beautiful plants, I saw Jesus walking towards me. As usual, He was wearing a long, white robe. He embraced me as a father hugs his daughter. He said nothing as we walked around. I was literally inhaling nature. Then Jesus hugged me a second time; it was so comforting and reassuring. I woke up with these words on my mind: "You have just been in paradise." I was so happy and extremely grateful for this experience of walking in the garden with Jesus. My gratitude for nature rose to a new level. I begin to appreciate nature and started looking at things differently.

A Grateful Heart

A grateful heart attracts good things, and you become a magnet to attract favour and blessings.
A grateful heart opens doors to favour.
Favour is better than riches.
Favour can open any door, but the rich pay their way through every door.

I remember giving a friend a gift one day, and I quickly scribbled words of encouragement on a scrap of paper. It probably took me a minute to write it down; what surprised me was that it was unplanned, and I was so surprised when

I read it myself. I believe that it was inspired by the Holy Spirit, as I felt a burst of inspiration.

A Blessing for You

May the sun release the sunshine in you.
May your smile give a glimpse of hope.
May your footsteps show the way forward.
May your character lead the way.
May your faith promote the gospel.
May favour and blessings become your weapons,
And may your gratitude light up a room.

Resources

1. Scripture quotations are from the *Holy Bible New King James Version*, Copyright 1990, by Thomas Nelson Inc.
2. *Holy Bible New International Version* (NIV) Copyright 1973, 1978, 1984, 2011 by Biblica, used by permission.
3. Internet sources:
   www.dictionary.com
   www.merriam-webster dictionary.

Book Summary

Faith—It's Voice Activated is to help other believers on their spiritual journeys to discover and appreciate that life is a process. We must recognise that we need a relationship with Jesus, and not religion.

For me, an encounter with Jesus was the beginning of a new relationship with Him. God will interrupt our plans when we least expect it and if we fail to acknowledge Him.

In *Faith—It's Voice Activated*, I have shared a few of my visions/dreams from Jesus and related how these have impacted my life. It's my personal journey of revelation in knowing the Creator. I briefly discuss my journey of faith and relationship with the Holy Spirit. We all need visions and dreams, and I sincerely hope this book will help you to activate your faith by speaking it out. May you grow closer to God and take your relationship to another spiritual level of intimacy with our Father.

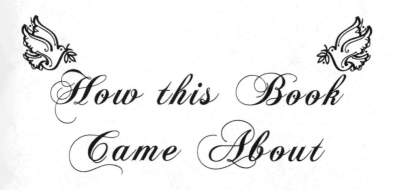

How this Book Came About

An encounter with God while I was in my car changed the course of my life. My personal relationship with Jesus started all over that day. God interrupted my plans, and I recommitted my life to Him. As my faith grew, Jesus showed more of Himself to me through revelation. This book is based on my personal revelations. I was hungry to know more, and the Holy Spirit became my best friend.

As I got the answers to my questions, I was totally in awe of how God used simple things like songs, scripture, or people to give me these answers. I continue to ask questions, because life is a process, and my faith grows daily. The grace of God is new every day. The Christian life is not meant to be easy. There will always be trials and temptations, but if you know who you are in Christ, you will be able to stand when things get tough.

Printed in the United States
By Bookmasters